2

Immaculate Heart of Mother Mary

Jennifer Ruth Russell

Disclaimer
The information in this book, and all information written or channeled by Jennifer Ruth Russell in any manner or form, is not intended or implied to be a substitute for professional health or medical advice, diagnosis or treatment, or for professional financial advice. Health, financial and life results vary with each individual and no results are guaranteed. No writing from Jennifer Ruth Russell is meant or intended to diagnose, treat, cure or prevent any disease or other life condition.

I

Contents

Forward

I have been waiting to bring this information to Lightworkers for some time. Jennifer's willingness to be the open channel and her determination to be an epicenter of financial healing and ascension is the perfect combination to present this now.

Mother Sophia has always provided everything for her beloved children. Mankind has been toiling in a barren field for so long. This field is of your own making and doesn't produce an everlasting harvest.

It is time to come back into the fullness of Her embrace. To lay down your arms of struggle from your little self and surrender into the tender love and intimacy of Her lavish care.

The table has been laid out with the finest china; utensils of pure gold and goblets of pure diamond and jeweled crystals. The table is always full of all that you'd ever desire.

Come and sup with me here until you are full of remembrance of your true divine nature.

You will remember that you are a powerful co-creator and master of energy. Nothing in this world has any power over you.

This book is an invitation to the banquet of your true Wealth and Abundance. Through the Union of our Hearts you will be healed of the misperceptions of lack and limitation.

I love and adore you,
Mother Mary

About this Book

This book is the culmination of an inquiry that began a decade ago. Being a student of the Seven Sacred Flames, I was intrigued by one of the qualities of the 5th Ray of Healing and Manifestation; "Abundance flows from the Immaculate Heart of Mary." (Seven Sacred Flames by Aurelia Louise Jones).

Little did I know that this question would lead me down a path of intimate mentorship with Mother Mary. She has healed my heart, my life and my finances.

Mother Mary asked me to step up and be her voice in helping those working in the Light to take dominion in their money life.

I was literally put on notice a week before my mini course *21 Day Abundance Activation with Mother Mary* began. Mother Mary and the Angels of Abundance* wanted to download a message for each day of the course and make it into a book.

21 Days to Abundance through the Immaculate Heart of Mother Mary was birthed in the stillness of the Union of our Hearts. She is answering the urgent call from Lightworkers for a new paradigm of wealthy spiritual leadership.

*The Angels of Abundance are brilliant Gold and serve on the 10th Ray of Infinite Abundance and Eternal Peace. They are here to help mankind lift up out of the old heaviness of debt, shame, guilt, unworthiness, undeservedness and fear that has become our experience of money and into our true inheritance of spiritual wealth. Whenever I call on Mother Mary the Angels of Abundance always come with her, surrounding her in radiant Golden Light.

How to use this Book

The ultimate way to use this book is as a complement to the mini course 21 Day Abundance Activation with Mother Mary.
https://angelsofabundanceascensionacademy.com/21-day/

Alternatively at any time, set aside 21 days and read one message a day in sequential order. This is an intimate process that Mother Mary and the Angels of Abundance will be taking you through one glorious step at a time. Have your journal handy.

After you've completed the 21 days, continue to strengthen your heart union with Mother Mary by coming back to the chapters that call to you. This new approach to the flow of Abundance may take some time to integrate into your life. Or if you like, randomly choose a number between 1 and 21 and take that day's message for your daily spiritual practice.

Day 1

You are a Mighty Force

Welcome Beloved we will be leading you, gently nudging you to receive your true inheritance of wealth and the flow of Abundance. This gift flows through my pure heart. Live through my heart, beloved, for it is expansive. I will show you the way to open this flow.

I love the will of the Father and the spaciousness of the Mother. I represent Her, we all do, for She is Grace, the Holy Spirit of the Divine Feminine Christ within you.

Allow yourself to be nurtured. You are a mighty force here and we want to empower you to do the work you came here to do. We want you to feel the flow of this work and financial freedom at the same time. For many of you have separated the two. It is time for them to come together as one for you and for everyone that you touch.

You are leading the way for many. Thank you for your presence and your attention.

I love and adore you,
Mother Mary and the Angels of Abundance

Day 2

Graft your Heart to Mine

Beloved you must come into my heart in order to experience the flow of Abundance. Abundance flows from my Immaculate Heart.

Come with a child like faith and allow your heart to open to me. I have been holding your Immaculate Concept for your entire existence. I see you as the Perfection of Divinity. I can't see you any other way.

Today, I want you to graft your heart to mine. Keep this very simple. Let the precious Christ Child within your heart come and be one with my heart. Close your eyes and let the breath help you to do this.

Come into your innocence. 'Let me be your Mother'*. Breathe here and rest here in my heart.

We begin here with allowing your heart to become one with mine.

Today, let yourself be a precious Child of God. Embrace your innocence. It is enough. You are enough.

In fact it is all you'll ever need to take dominion in every area of your life - including your financial well being.

I love and adore you,
Mother Mary and the Angels of Abundance

* Memoirs of Beloved Jesus and Mother Mary by Werner Schroeder

Day 3

Your Heart is the Instrument of Abundance

Beloved, take the time everyday to continue to come into communion with me and my Immaculate Heart. For it is Purity itself. I will help your heart to come back to its original blueprint of being a pure open vessel.

This is important because your heart is the instrument of Abundance. It is where your Divine inheritance of Opulence lives.

As you lift your thoughts into the union of our hearts, feel my Presence. Allow me to fill your heart with the feeling of Abundance. It will be individually tailored for you. Be open to whatever Abundance feels like and looks like.

Do this often so you can sense if you are in Abundance or out of Abundance. There is really only one or the other.

Ask your Angels of Abundance to help you with this.

Today, as you are going about your day pause often and check in with your heart. Are you in the flow of Abundance or out of the flow? Keep this very simple. If you are out, ask me to help you get back into the expansive feeling of Abundance.

I love and adore you,
Mother Mary and the Angels of Abundance

Day 4

Your Mighty Beloved I AM Presence

Beloved, when I ask you to graft your heart to mine, you must do this from your High Holy Self, your Mighty Victorious I AM PRESENCE. This is your Divinity. This is your Eternal Being in God.

You can only access true Abundance from your Beloved I AM Presence. Your smaller self will continue in the old ways of suffering, manipulation and lack, trying to create out of the substance of the world.

Your Beloved I AM Presence gives you Divine Authority. It is why you are a powerful Christed being.

When you call on me from your I AM THAT I AM, it brings you into your right alignment and allows our hearts to meld and become ONE from the highest place possible.

You are not lesser than me. We are equals. I simply operate from an Ascended state, from a high-level of Love Light and Authority. That's why when you graft your heart to mine, everything from my dimension is available to you.

Here's a simple way to connect our hearts:

Simply say: *"In the name I AM THAT I AM I call upon Mother Mary. I command my heart to meld with her Immaculate Heart and the flow of Abundance. And so it is".*

I love and adore you,
Mother Mary and the Angels of Abundance

Day 5

Stay in the Eternal Now

Beloved, when you sync your heart with mine it helps you to stay in the Eternal Now.

The flow of Abundance, as well as every Perfect gift, is always in the Eternal Now. An Abundant life is the Father's will for you and the Mother's deepest desire for you, Her precious child.

When you see portraits of me around the world you will usually see me in an outer robe of blue with a red garment closest to my heart and body.

The blue symbolizes the love that I have for the will of Father God. The will of God in every Eternal Moment is for your highest and best good. It is the perfect plan for you and for your role in expanding the Light of Heaven.

The red symbolizes the open hearted love and nurturing of the Divine Mother.

Your heart houses your Beloved I AM Presence, it is where the Kingdom Queendom of God resides within you. It is your glorious and simple center of the Universe.

The reason that I am looking down in most of my portraits (I had a lot to do with these paintings), is my desire to stay in the Eternal Now and to listen to the promptings of my heart. This allowed me to stay in a state of listening grace so I wouldn't miss one subtle moment of instruction.

If you are feeling stressed about your financial situation - your human mind is pulling you into the future or back into the past.

Do your best to keep your heart in sync with mine and the Angels of Abundance. Stay in the Eternal Now. Listen for the instructions that will help you stay in the frequency of Abundance and what you need to do right now.

Take only the instructions of your heart in this Eternal Now.

I love and adore you,
Mother Mary and the Angels of Abundance

Day 6

The Union of our Hearts is a Vortex

Beloved, the definition of a vortex, in your language, is a whirl of water or air, or the center of something that draws the outside in.

Consider the grafting of our hearts as a mighty center, a powerful vortex, of Abundance. Your Divine Inheritance of Abundance can easily flow from here.

See the dam of lack and resistance, being broken open so that every bit of supply that is yours is finally opened and allowed to flow.

The power of our heart union defies all logic. Use your imagination to feel the pull of our heart union. You are able to literally draw down from the 10th Golden Ray, Infinite Abundance, Eternal Peace and the God Supply of all that is Good*. See it rushing to you. Imagine it increasing within the vortex. Feel it taking over your heart and your subtle bodies.

You literally have to pull this down. By your intention, claim it and *command* it. Your voice, is the vehicle to do this.

"Through my Beloved I AM Presence I claim my Divine inheritance NOW! I command that Infinite Abundance flows through the union of my heart with the Immaculate Heart of Mother Mary. It

flows easily to me NOW. I receive it. I allow myself to have what is already mine. (See the vortex opening even wider)

I request that this vortex of Abundance be established and sustained within me now and forever more.

I am grateful that I am always fully supplied in whatever I require to fulfill my soul's purpose.

And so it is! Beloved I AM!"

I love and adore you,
Mother Mary and the Angels of Abundance

* *I AM CoCreating the New Earth* – Patricia Cota-Robles,
The Era of Peace

Day 7

Healing Money Wounds

Beloved, as you are getting familiar with the union of our hearts and power of this vortex, you are ready to start purifying your experience with money.

Even if you are in what appears to be an ocean of human consciousness of lack and scarcity, you can create an island of plenty.

You can vibrationally establish your own experience of money.

When anyone is connected with me their heart begins to heal on every level. As we are getting closer and closer together, your heart will be revealing past traumas to you. It's time to release them and transmute them back into the Light.

Since we are focusing on Abundance, I urge you to invite your old money wounds to surface and transmute them within the union of our hearts.

Let yourself feel the emotional pain of these memories and wash them clean in the union of our hearts with the New Rosary.

"Hail Mary full of Grace
The Lord is with Thee
O Sacred Heart of the Mother Flame
Hold the Immaculate Vision for me (us)
Precious Child (Sons and Daughters) of the Most High

Holy Ma-Ray, Queen of Angels
Hear my (our) call for wholeness
Pray for me (us) now
In my (our) Victory, my (our) Perfection and my (our) Ascension
*fulfilled"**

Continue to speak this prayer until your heart is cleansed.

I love you and adore you,
Mother Mary and the Angels of Abundance

* Prayer inspired by Elizabeth Claire Prophet and Patricia Cota-Robles

Day 8

Clearing the Past

Beloved, today I want you to focus on clearing the past.

It's time to come into the Eternal Now by forgiving everything and everyone.

The pain of the past wants to be purified in your heart and it is taking up space in your heart and the vitality of your life.

You have the power to do this and I urge you to do it today and every day.

Forgiveness increases the momentum of Love Light in your life and in the union of our hearts. It opens the Abundance vortex even wider.

Begin by connecting with your Beloved I AM Presence and then call upon me, my son the Ascended Jesus Christ, the Angels of Abundance and the Archangels of the Violet Flame, Archangel Zadkiel and Holy Amethyst to assist you.

Command your freedom from the past.

Do a scan of your life and ask for every hidden resentment, blame, judgment, criticism and un-forgiveness to be revealed to you. Write them down in a list.

Speak a simple prayer of forgiveness over each one and turn it over to the Holy Spirit to undo it at the very source, the place where it began.

Then speak a blessing for that person or situation.

Make sure you feel the release in your heart. If you don't, pray again and repeat this simple process.

Keep this simple, but do a thorough job of it Beloved. Be generous with your forgiveness.

"For they know not what they do" ~ Jeshua

You can do this.

I love and adore you,
Mother Mary and the Angels of Abundance

Day 9

Restore your Innocence

Beloved come into my heart, sink deeply into my love and forgive yourself. Forgive yourself everything.

Today I'm asking you to come back into your innocence. For you are blameless.

Stop blaming yourself or anyone else for where you are financially. Let yourself off the hook for everything that has happened.

There is nothing wrong with you Beloved. And you have not done it wrong.

I'm asking you to reclaim the power of your innocence.

This will help you to be bold in all of your interactions. It will help you to lift up into the high value of your worth and charge a good amount of money for your time and spiritual gifts.

It will open up your mind to receive the brilliance of direction from Divine Mind to bring about your true Wealth and Abundance.

It will also help you to see others in their innocence. This will help your relationships come into harmony.

Come into the vortex, the union of our hearts and call on me and the Angels of Abundance to help you reclaim the sovereign power of your innocence and forgive yourself everything.

Sing the Ho'oponopono Prayer Chant to yourself often.

https://youtu.be/dq_5VyobIYo

I love and adore you,
Mother Mary and the Angels of Abundance

Day 10

Purify your Money

Beloved as you keep opening up your heart and grafting it with my Sacred Heart, it is opening up a pathway of Abundance for you.

Keep purifying your own heart with forgiveness and love. Keep it pristine. There is always an opportunity in every Eternal moment to begin again. Be gentle in this process.

I am always right here holding the Immaculate Concept for you and our Holy Union.

You are ready now to begin to purify your money and all your money affairs. Money is like the air and the water. It is of the elemental kingdom wanting to come back to the Light. And your money has been put in your care. Money itself has been treated very poorly by mankind.

Make this a daily practice and do it in this manner.

Establish the Union of our Hearts and invoke the assistance of Lord Zadkiel and Holy Amethyst and your Angels of Abundance to bring the full power of the Violet Flame into the Union of our Hearts.

See the vortex that we are building, filled with this stream of Living Consciousness. This is pure Divine Alchemy. This Violet Ray is the gift of this Age of Aquarius and it is a Mighty efficient cleanser. It is the Ray of Freedom. It transmutes all shadow into Light.

Now bring all of the money in your life, in whatever form it is, through the vortex. See the elementals in the metal of the coins, in the paper, and in digital form being washed in the Violet Flame.

Continue to do this with every thought and activity around your money. Every bill received, every time you go to pay a bill, every transaction of exchange, every debt and every thought about your money - purify it in the Violet Flame and bless it.

"Violet Flame, Violet Flame, Violet Flame, blaze, blaze, blaze through all of my money, transmuting all shadow into Light, Light, Light."

It is important that you refrain from all financial transactions unless you are in this state of purity.

Give the elementals within the circulation of money a chance to spread the Light of Freedom wherever they go.

After you do this for your personal money, send this blessing out to all the money in the world.

I love and adore you,
Mother Mary and the Angels of Abundance

Day 11

Dissolve the Burden of Debt

Beloved, today we are going to continue releasing that which doesn't serve your true Wealth and Abundance.

As you build the momentum of the Violet Flame into the vortex of our hearts with all of your activity around money, don't hesitate to bring in the burden of your debt.

There is more debt in your world then money. It is like a dark cloud over most of humankind.

It doesn't matter how much debt that you have right now. What matters is how you think and feel about it and taking back your power around it.

I'm asking you to purify this area of your life within the Union of our Hearts.

Allow yourself to feel into your debt. Get inside the very essence of it. What does it feel like and look like? Simply allow it to be what it is.

Now take dominion of it with your decision of what you'd like it to be. Lighten it up; see it dissolving in the Violet Flame. Ask the Angels of Abundance to help you dissolve the burden of it in your life.

Do this as often as is needed until the hold your debt has over you is released. Let this be as easy as washing the dishes.

Be open and ready to listen to any guidance that you will be receiving regarding what is yours to do about your debt.

I love and adore you,
Mother Mary and the Angels of Abundance

Day 12

Guard your Emotions

Beloved, I'm asking you to be vigilant with your feeling tone. It is a marker of the purity of your auric field.

You will be healing emotionally because your heart is one with mine. The trauma of betrayal, of rejection, of lack will be asking for forgiveness and healing. Welcome this healing and let us purify it together.

As your frequency of Light becomes higher and higher; everything will be attracted to your Light, just like moths to a flame.

Notice when there is a disturbance within our heart union, this vortex of Light we are building. Do your best not to brush it off and ignore it. Be vigilant in your feeling tone and take care of it.

Think of any activity of shadow as impersonal, as a distortion of the Light asking to be freed.

Being in public can make you susceptible to taking on shadow in your auric field. This could happen while talking to someone on the phone. It could also happen with old patterns of your own thoughts.

Lack is shadow.

If you find yourself feeling off, call in the Violet Flame, through your Beloved I AM Presence, as we did in Day 8. *Command* your freedom of all shadow in the Light. Ask for all shadow to be transmuted back to pure Light until your auric field is completely purified.

As your emotional body becomes stronger it will be able to hold the frequency of Abundance even if you are in a sea of scarcity and fear.

Ask Beloved Archangel Michael to completely shield you in Divine Protection as you get stronger and stronger in the Light.

I love and adore you,
Mother Mary and the Angels of Abundance

Day 13

What was my Agreement?

Beloved, you made an agreement before you came of what you wanted your experience of money to be in this world, this time around.

Some of you were so intent on doing your part in Earth's Ascension, that you didn't plan for your own provision.

Many of you have become distracted from your work because of your financial situation.

The good news is you can change it now.

Spend some time today in this inquiry.

Connect with your Beloved I AM Presence and your Beloved team. Connect with my heart by invoking my Presence and the Angels of Abundance and ask the question: *"What was my agreement around my experience of money during this lifetime?"* *
Be open to whatever you hear and write it down.

Have a conversation with me about it. I'm right here with you.

When Jennifer asked this question the answer she received was startling to her in its starkness. "You didn't make any plans for your experience of money...nothing."

Whatever you hear, use it as an opportunity to love yourself even more.

I love and adore you,
Mother Mary and the Angels of Abundance

* Adapted from Abundance for All by Caroline Oceana
Ryan

Day 14

Your Agreement in the Eternal Now

Beloved, the intimacy of this little book began with Jennifer's experience of receiving the answer to her inquiry that she made no plan for her experience with money in this lifetime.

I've asked her to share this beginning because I think it will be helpful for you in re-writing your own Agreement.

After she heard 'nothing' her heart immediately opened in forgiveness to her Eternal Self. "Beloved, you had no idea what it would be like here, in this time, without an agreement of prosperity."

As she thought about what she wanted to change in her agreement, she turned to me and asked if she could borrow my Immaculate Agreement until hers became strong enough.

This began the grafting of our hearts together in this deep way. And after years of trying to change her experience with money, she released it into the union of our hearts.

Beloved, I would be glad to do this for you as well. The actions that you've tried around your experience of prosperity have had a small effect and changed very little in your life.

I'm calling you to lift up to a whole new level of your true Wealth and Abundance. I'm inviting you to receive as you never have before. You weren't meant to do this alone.

What is your new money agreement?

Ask for what you need and the Angels of Abundance and I would be more than glad to help you with it. We can't assist you without you formally asking.

We'll never take away the 'learning' that your Soul has planned for you. But we can show you the way and literally hold your hand as you walk across this bridge of freedom, out of lack and into Abundance.

I love and adore you,
Mother Mary and the Angels of Abundance

Day 15

Your Commitment

Beloved, you weren't drawn to me and this little book by accident. Your path has been perfectly designed.

You have been seeking your true Wealth and Abundance for a while now and I want to assure you that it is part of your Ascension journey.

Now that you have changed your agreement with your experience of money in this world, I'm now going to ask you to make a firm commitment to stay in this new agreement, every moment of every day.

As you change the ruts in your conscious and subconscious mind your commitment is essential to bringing it about in the physical world.

Just as your decision to ascend must be met by your daily commitment towards it, so it is with this new agreement. It will not happen without your conscious intent.

Every bit of conscious commitment on your part is fully met by the Company of Heaven. We rush to assist those who have committed to their own mastery and amplify it.

You have asked for this kind of discipline. You not only asked for this initiation into your true Wealth and Abundance, you wanted to prove to yourself that you could do this.

You can do this Beloved. As you are grafting your heart to mine it will be simple and doable to stay focused, in faith, and committed to your new agreement.

Take the time to write out your new agreement and place it on your altar. Affirm it often.

I love and adore you,
Mother Mary and the Angels of Abundance

Day 16

Bask Often in the Ray of Abundance

Beloved, today I want to invite you to bask often in the Ray of Abundance.

Abundance is a gift from God. You don't have to do anything for it. Simply receive it.

Abundance is. It can't be divided, diminished, or destroyed because it's part of the Godhead.

Remember that any other thought or appearance otherwise is an illusion and doesn't exist.

Come Beloved and let's lift up together into the Holy Golden Light.

Call on your Beloved I AM Presence to radiate this Golden Sun within your Heart. Let it emanate throughout your entire body. Breathe deeply ... this will help distribute the Flame into every cell, atom and electron of your auric field.

Now ask me and the Angels of Abundance to amplify it and increase your feeling of Abundance.

"I AM ABUNDANCE. ABUNDANCE I AM."

Command it to expand, expand, expand, increasing the Golden Light until you feel you are completely ONE.

Now let's ask the Holy Spirit and Beloved Vesta to increase the frequency within you even more. Breathe, breathe, breathe! Receive, receive, receive!

Lift up higher and higher in this Golden Ray of Infinite Abundance and Eternal Peace until it consumes you. Stay here and bask in the glory of your true nature.

When you feel complete, let Abundance radiate out from you right into the center of Virgo our planetary Goddess. Then encircling the globe until the entire world is consumed in this Golden Ray.

Let the Golden Light of Abundance become your feeling tone. This is your home. Bask here often.

Thank you for lifting your frequency and all of mankind into Abundance.

I love and adore you,
Mother Mary and the Angels of Abundance

Day 17

"Give and to you shall be given" ~ Jeshua

Beloved, every good thing flows to you. As you receive, fully receive - and then give it.

As you are always Sourced from Father Mother through your Beloved I AM Presence, it is important to build your faith in this by giving of your money.

The Law of the Circle is always in motion asking you to participate in the inflow and the outflow. Money is God energy and it must move.

Watch yourself and see where you are withholding your money. Where are you hoarding in fear that your supply will run out? Just like water and air, money must be in motion. Don't let your money stagnate.

Be generous with yourself and with others.

As you come within our Heart Union see where you have been spiritually nurtured this week. Give your money there. Even if you feel that you are starting to grip in fear ... give in thankfulness, expecting the gift to return to you multiplied.

As you continue to participate in giving back to Source in appreciation for the gift of your life, stay open to receive on the return current. Watch as the Law of the Circle multiplies all that you require to live well.

Without giving, you will not be participating in the Abundant flow of the Universe. As you give freely, it will be freely given.

This will also build your faith. Your faith is pure Gold. It's money in the bank.

You are always fully supplied. Prove this to yourself and let go Beloved. Let go of the clutching and allow yourself to participate in this limitless Circle of Life.

I love and adore you,
Mother Mary and the Angels of Abundance

Day 18

The Glory of your Ascension

Beloved, I know your heart intimately. When your body was being formed in the womb, you came to my Temple of the Sacred Heart above Fatima. I carefully knitted the very fabric of your heart from a high rarified Substance of the Christ Consciousness.

That's why we are intimately connected at all times.

My Sacred Heart is a pathway of Light for you. Abundance flows from my Heart and Abundance is a natural part of your Ascension.

Before I was the mother of Jesus, I had many lifetimes. I went through the process of transcending the pain of separation, lack and death as you are doing.

As you lift up into the Union of our Hearts, see yourself lifting up through this pathway of Light, transcending everything of this Earth. You are here to remember how to do this.

See yourself lifting up into your Light body, your Beloved I AM Presence, and becoming One.

Let yourself go beyond your human mind and understanding and step into the Glory of your Ascension.

Ascension is the Divine Marriage of your human self and your Beloved I AM Presence.

Seeking Abundance without intending to Ascend is futile. It will keep you Earth bound and in the struggle of mankind.

Allow me and the Angels of Abundance to assist you in your Ascension.

I love and adore you,
Mother Mary and the Angels of Abundance

Day 19

Command your Healing Now

Beloved, I am the Archaii on the 5th Ray, the Emerald Green Ray, of Healing and Manifestation.

When you call upon me thousands of Angels and Elementals come with me, including my Twin Flame Archangel Raphael, to assist you. There is a huge collective in my healing field.

Today I want you to focus on your own financial healing. For this is the gift that I bring to you and there is no reason that you need suffer any longer.

Many of you have had lifetimes of spiritual service which mistakenly has brought with it ancient vows of poverty and silence.

To go without and to suffer was considered to be an honorable and holy endeavor.

Today these old vows can show up as unworthiness and guilt. Do you feel unworthy to receive a fair exchange of money for your spiritual gifts and time? And when money does come in ... do you feel guilty receiving it?

There is a lot of guilt around actually having. This causes you to continue to put the brakes on your financial flow.

Let's heal this now Beloved.

It's important that you command your healing of this old pattern of unworthiness and guilt.

The 5th Ray is also a channel of Truth. Truth is the beginning of all healing.

The Truth about you as a servant of the Most High is that you are always fully provided for. That includes; full to overflowing bank accounts, little or no debt, beautiful vacations, enjoyment, relaxation and times of renewal.

The Truth of the Kingdom of Heaven is Opulence not poverty.

Command this Truth for your life now. *Insist* on your financial healing.

Take some time today to formally call on me. Gaze into my eyes as you listen to my keynote, the song, Ave Marie and come into the vastness of our heart connection. Feel the Healing Collective of Angels, your Abundance Angels and Elementals surrounding you. Ask the vortex of healing to increase in intensity and size until you feel completely saturated and surrounded by the Emerald Green Ray.

Then say: "I *Command financial wholeness NOW*. I *Command my Freedom NOW*.

Holy Spirit undo at the source, all guilt around having money, conscious and unconscious.

I claim it done, it is finished NOW. And so it is!"

Come as often as you need to heal this Beloved, for you are worthy of every good thing.

I love and adore you,
Mother Mary and the Angels of Abundance

Day 20

The Art of Having

Beloved, are you allowing yourself to desire? This is an important part of creation. If you don't desire, how can you intend?

Your intention is creative and when it is backed by a desire it fuels manifestation.

See your desires as Holy. For they are not only planted within your heart by Beloved Father Mother, they also sharpen your manifestation skills.

You are absolutely *allowed* to have a healthy income. You are absolutely *allowed* to have work that you love. You are absolutely *allowed* to have lots of love in your life. You are absolutely *allowed* to have whatever you require to be happy and healthy. Really, you are absolutely *allowed* to have anything you desire.

I can feel your heart start to tense up by these words. Breathe with me, feel into your heart and find the resistance.

Have you desired something for so long and nothing has come of it? Have you been disappointed over and over again and have decided it's not worth it to desire?

Call on your Beloved I AM Presence and bring the resistance into the Union of our Hearts. Ask me and the Angels of Abundance to cleanse this desire back to its original spark. Purify it in the Golden Light of Abundance.

Ask a few simple questions. *"What have I learned by not having the fulfillment of this desire?", "Is my learning complete?"* Write down your answers. Continue to ask questions until you get back to the purity of this desire. Forgive everything, especially yourself.

As you give yourself permission to have this desire, the desire itself will bring you the skills of manifestation and the artistry of having.

Your job is to continue to hold it fresh before you. Continue to allow yourself to desire and focus toward this desire until it is fulfilled. It won't happen without you.

Love this desire. Sing to it. Let your whole body harmonize with it. Become one with your desire.

You can do this Beloved. It is your life in motion. You are cultivating the art of having.

I love and adore you,
Mother Mary and the Angels of Abundance

Day 21

Let the Dance Continue

Beloved, I love and adore you. When I look at you, I only see your Immaculate Concept, the Perfection of your being. You are Radiance Itself.

Let's continue this Dance of Abundance together. We have just begun and the pathway of Light that we have created in the Union of our Hearts will continue to widen and deepen, if you so desire.

There is a capacity of great Abundance to flow from this pathway of Light. As you allow me to help heal your heart from the pain of not having and feeling like you are not enough, this vortex will open up more and more.

The money system of this world is dissolving and disintegrating. Don't waste your time trying to figure it out in the physical.

Continue to draw close to me and graft your heart to mine as often as you can, for we are moving past the system that you know. It is corrupt and not in the Divine Plan for the New Earth.

What would you like the new system to be? The ideas that flow from you are important to create the New World. You are part of what is being created. Give yourself time to dream and visualize often. *What would you enjoy? What would you like the exchange of energy to be?*

You are literally creating your reality. Have fun with this. Write out your vision of true Wealth and Abundance. Writing something down and looking at the words that you've created often, makes them so.

Come dance in the Light with me as often as you can. The Angels of Abundance and I can literally help to lift you into the frequency of Abundance anytime.

We love and adore you,
Mother Mary and the Angels of Abundance

Dedication

I dedicate this book to my brothers and sisters who are on the mystical journey. To those of you who love God so much that the call of your heart is greater than anything in this world.

My beloved family of Light may you no longer suffer in lack or limitation, worry or fear.

May you step into your power as a wealthy Light Engineer in this unprecedented time of rapid reconstruction of our world.

We need you now more than ever before.

I created the Angels of Abundance Ascension Academy because I am passionate about empowering Holistic Healers, Ministers, Practitioners and students of Light to become strong spiritually and financially.
Mother Mary and I'd love to continue this journey with you.

In Love and Joyful Abundance,

Jennifer

AngelsofAbundanceAscensionAcademy.com

Purchase Jennifer's award winning songs and recordings here:
http://jenniferruthrussell.com/music/

Acknowledgements

I give thanks for the gentle insistence of Mother Mary and the Angels of Abundance to download these powerful messages that is helping us change the paradigm of spiritual wealth for Energy Healers.

I am grateful for the precious Family of Light of the Angels of Abundance Ascension Academy for calling this book forward and for completing the circle of this inquiry.

I give thanks for all the teachers that have gone before me and influenced my journey of true Wealth and Abundance: Jeshua, Saint Germain, Archangel Michael, Metatron, Godfrey King, Ronna Herman, Auriela Louise Jones, Patricia Cota-Robles, Caroline Oceana Ryan, the Sophia Dragon Tribe Mentors and Kaia Ra, the I AM Discourses, the Bridge to Freedom work, Catherine Ponder, Ernest Holmes, Eric Butterworth, John Randolph Price, Elizabeth Clare Prophet, Michael Bernard Beckwith, Rev. Margaret Shepherd, Lynn Twist, Vrinda Normand, Rev. Jennifer Hadley and Rev. Karen Russo.

I give thanks to my beloved prayer partner Taffy Wallace who continually reminds me of who I am.

I give thanks to Michelle Walker for her joyful creation of Mother Mary that adorns the front cover of this book and her friendship. I give thanks for the Awesome out-of-the-box Goddess mastermind group that always calls me to think higher.

Special thanks to Susanne James for lovingly keeping me within the lines by editing this little book and Elizabeth

MacFarland, my graphic designer who always brings a sparkle of excellence to everything.

I am grateful for my son Andy and my entire family who continues to show me what unconditional love is.

I am extremely grateful for my beloved husband and partner Michael Gayle who always supports everything I do, produces all of my music and brings sunshine into my life every day.

About the Author

Jennifer has been a Spiritual Mentor for more than 16 years. She trained at Agape International Spiritual Center, in Culver City, California, under Rev. Michael Bernard Beckwith. She has mentored thousands of clients and students in the depths of financial lack and heartache, helping them to heal their hearts and lives by connecting to the Light of their own Divinity.

Jennifer is the creator of Angels of Abundance Ascension Academy. This year long study into the Mysteries of the Higher Realms empowers students to become the healers they came here to be, emerging as an oracle of guidance for themselves and others.

Her intimate partnership with Mother Mary, Archangel Michael, Saint Germain and the entire Company of Heaven is the unseen force that runs the Ascension Academy.

Jennifer is also an award winning songwriter. Songs have always poured out of her heart. She loves to take people into the stillness of the soul and the playfulness of the light. She has written and recorded eleven CDs, including her award winning Virtues Songs A-Z for children.

Jennifer's life vision is to uplift and empower Lightworkers to live abundantly, and transform the world with songs and prayers that open the heart. When you are in her presence you will feel the deep connection of the Angels.

"A moment with Jennifer is like immersing yourself in the inspiration of the best music and the love of a most powerful prayer."
– Rev. Michael Bernard Beckwith

Made in the USA
San Bernardino, CA
08 June 2018